Where We Start

THE DREAMSEEKER
POETRY SERIES

Books in the DreamSeeker Poetry Series, intended to make available fine writing by Anabaptist-related poets, are published by Cascadia Publishing House under the DreamSeeker Books imprint and often copublished with Herald Press. Cascadia oversees content of these poetry collections in collaboration with DreamSeeker Poetry Series Editor Jean Janzen as well as in consultation with its Editorial Council and the authors themselves.

1. On the Cross
   By Dallas Wiebe, 2005
2. I SAW GOD DANCING
   By Cheryl Denise Miller, 2005
3. Evening Chore
   By Shari Wagner, 2005
4. Where We Start
   By Debra Gingerich, 2007

Also worth noting are two poetry collections that would likely have been included in the series had it been in existence then:

1. Empty Room with Light
   By Ann Hostetler, 2002
2. A Liturgy for Stones
   By David Wright, 2003

Where We Start

Poetry by
Debra Gingerich

DreamSeeker Poetry Series, Volume 4

DreamSeeker Books
TELFORD, PENNSYLVANIA

an imprint of
Cascadia Publishing House

Copublished with
Herald Press
Scottdale, Pennsylvania

Cascadia Publishing House orders, information, reprint permissions:
contact@CascadiaPublishingHouse.com
1-215-723-9125
126 Klingerman Road, Telford PA 18969
www.CascadiaPublishingHouse.com

Where We Start
Copyright © 2007 by Cascadia Publishing House, Telford, PA 18969
All rights reserved
DreamSeeker Books is an imprint of Cascadia Publishing House
Copublished with Herald Press, Scottdale, PA
Library of Congress Catalog Number: 2006027817
ISBN 10: 1-931038-39-2; **ISBN-13:** 978-1-931038-39-3
Book design by Cascadia Publishing House
Cover design by Gwen M. Stamm

The paper used in this publication is recycled and meets the
minimum requirements of American National Standard for Information
Sciences—Permanence of Paper for Printed Library Materials, ANSI Z39.48-1984.1984

Library of Congress Cataloguing-in-Publication Data
Gingerich, Debra, 1968-
  Where we start : poems / by Debra Gingerich.
    p. cm. -- (Dreamseeker poetry series ; v. 4)
  ISBN-13: 978-1-931038-39-3 (trade pbk. : alk. paper)
  ISBN-10: 1-931038-39-2 (trade pbk. : alk. paper)
  I. Title.
PS3607.I457W48 2007
811'.6--dc22

                                          2006027817

14 13 12 11 10 09 08 07   10 9 8 7 6 5 4 3 2 1

For my parents,
Emanuel and Margaret;
and for Zvonko's parents,
Hasan and Radmila

CONTENTS

III: LOSING GROUND

I
PULLING TAFFY

Fairytale

Don't get distracted by fluff or filler, like the color of the step-mother's hair or the taste of the poison apple or your grand-mother drunk on mouthwash in her Iowa town. This isn't about your mother who FedExed a card for your wedding or the way she used to walk along train tracks—her arms spread open to embrace any oncoming mass. This isn't about the *God's my copilot* cousin who lifted your nightgown with licked fingers.

No, this is about your mattress—how you feel like the princess, swearing the problem's as small as a pea. About how you stick to recipes with cabbage or pig stomach. How you chase after your sanity, following breadcrumbs. This is about marrying a musician like your father—how a drum set's rhythm reminds you of the hoofs of a prince's horse. How it still took seven and a half years to say yes, and even now you're afraid a frog or beast will turn up somewhere. How you can't seem to find the proper ending to this story.

My Husband as a Child in Yugoslavia

The children have come out
after the hibernation season
with soccer balls left on lawns and bikes
sprawled up and down driveways.
He and his brother owned one bike,
his brother was bigger and not willing
to share. He says there are pictures
of him with flooded eyes,
pictures of him with crisp blond hair
in a soccer uniform in the truck
his father drove at the gold mine
or dressed up to play Cowboys
and Indians—taught through sub-titled TV
who was good and who was bad.
I have a heart-pendant necklace
made of the gold from that mine,
sent by a woman I do not know
who raised a boy to come
to America without packing
one childhood photo, as if he
was escaping a fire with just
a few clothes and books.
Every letter arrives from that country
with the slight scent of smoke.
It is no wonder he makes sure
the stove is turned off
each time he leaves the house.

Angel in the Blue Room

Identical tombstones outside Croghan
Mennonite Church line up
as if for role call, conservatively dressed
even in death. But my cousin's
is easily found in the back row engraved
A Child Shall Lead Them, and Eric did
travel before us in the months preceding
his death, small and weak enough
to be pushed ahead in a stroller
while my brother, the same age,
a lucky seven, played catch and croquet
in the front yard. Thirty people
miraculously squeezed through the narrow chamber
that Saturday afternoon we surrounded
the bed in the family farm's blue room.
Eric's mom whispered
Do you see the angels?
just hours after we had sent off
another cousin and his new wife
to their honeymoon cottage. Just before
the rest of us went to see
James Bond charm women, bullets,
and all of those high-tech gadgets
in order to save the world once more.
My parents didn't care that I was off
to watch skin and violence that matinee.
They knew better than to argue
with a place in the dark
where the mismatched ingredients
of that day could slip from my bones

for a makeshift moment, knew that soon enough
I'd return to blistering sunlight,
the blunt rays threading through
the pores of my scorched adolescence.

Lewis County Chronicle 1

Allen's younger brother cried
over leaving friends behind
in Baden, Ontario and his school
where he was learning multiplication.
But this was a town of too little land
and too many mouths,
too much competition
for cream hauling or cabinet making.
And Allen didn't imagine himself
as any better than his father.
What would a Mennonite man do
with knowledge more than
how to seed and milk
and read the German Bible?
A Mennonite man belonged
in his mother's hometown
with the cheap land and forests
in need of clearing,
a place where a large family
would be of use.
When they were met
at the Lowville, New York train depot
by his uncle in an auto, Allen even
stopped missing the team of horses
they had sold. Here his father would drive
a black Ford from which he'd wave
to every passerby to follow them home
from church for dinner. Here his father
would own a two hundred acre farm

with eighty milking cows to will to his sons,
along with his weak heart
and arteries that thickened
like cream churning to butter.

Newspaper Headline Reads: Sacrificial Sheep Shoves Man to his Death

What does one do
in a city as dense as Alexandria,
approaching the Eid al-Adha
feast of sacrifice, but keep
livestock in places like balconies
or basements? This fed-fat rooftop
sheep sensed such cohabitation
would lead nowhere

but to slaughter. In Tuzla,
Hasan must have feared
this too. Bosnian born, wife
from Serbia, sons given Croat
names, he took on the communist
cause—its red iron fist of unity.
These ten years after its downfall,
he still calls everyone comrade.

But his sons with rooftop views
scatter across countries and oceans,
marry women, eat food, speak languages
he'll never recognize. And what's left:
his house built stone upon stone, the sheep
he won't shear for fear he might
cut their skin, and a small fishing boat
willed to no one.

Grandfather Zehr's Schooling

He wouldn't let them sleep
when they arrived home late
after hitchhiking five hundred miles
from the nearest Mennonite college.
He'd fill the wood-burning cook stove
like it was time to warm the kitchen
for breakfast—their bags still resting
in the entryway—and quiz them on the view
in the planetarium, world geography,
even the fundamentals of physics
that make a plane fly—all that his
eighth-grade education had not provided.
Even the walk to bed was fueled
by discussions as they'd stumble
over Donna—still too young
to stay up past nine—hiding on the stairway
to overhear her brothers and father
debate underlined portions of text.
She would fight sleep, wording
"Psychiatrist" after her pre-med brother
or "Vietnam" from another's history class,
as if they were prayers. Then with the kids
in their beds and the flicker of his reading
lamp, he would milk every tired drop
out of a book about missionaries
in China, until he woke them at 5:00 a.m.
for chores and questions, their weary answers
a map to how they'd leave that farm for good.

Unsettled

It's been years since those full buckets of sap splashed the sides of my cold thighs, since Mom stood in the back yard, stirring the sugaring pot Dad cut from a thirty-gallon drum. It was my chore to collect drippings from neighbors' trees and later, set the bartered syrup on their doorsteps in emptied yogurt containers while I dreamed of the day in late winter when the end of last season's syrup rested on our Sunday pancakes—how I favored Mrs. Butterworth's dark candy pouring from that bottle I'd dress up into a grandma for my Barbies. I was a generation from the Sugar Bush—far enough to prefer store-bought over patience and fire. Years later, living in a rented city apartment, hardly caring to save potted plants, these claims of transformation uprooted themselves when my parents took me deep into the forest one spring day. We walked acres of stumps and wasted logs caused by a microburst storm, spinning wind and maples and me, wanting to scoop up the sap dripping from every broken limb.

Lewis County Chronicle 2

When needed at home, Marian
took a job sweeping the floor
of the one room schoolhouse
so she could read the students'
lessons left on the blackboard.
She would eavesdrop
when friends at church shared
their social studies assignments
and pretend the German lessons
in Sunday School led to a diploma.
She played evening games
of dominoes as if they were final
exams. Years later, in tight cursive
written to each of her eleven
grandchildren, she would admit,
"I did want to go to high school."
But it was sugaring season
and brother Sam had broken
an arm and no special treatment
could be given to a girl
born the ninth of eleven
on a Thursday in July
while her siblings visited
Grandmother Zehr
and the men finished haying.

Diversity

Mennonites know something
about beauty, though there may be
no hand-carved crucifix,
no gold-dipped Jesus, no colored glass
to pull the sun in, shining opaque
designs on carved cherry pews.
My uncle sings high and visible
in tenor, his head cocked slightly
to the right, as if the sound
is coming to him from above.
And I learned young that
I would never match my mother's
soprano, how it curved about
the voices in our country fellowship,
too small to be called a church.
I accepted alto and listened
for the sounds of other women
drifting below the melody,
like shadowing on a pencil sketch.
No one had to tell me
that God somehow can hear,
that he loves four-part harmony.
Otherwise, voices could never
fit together like that. And when
the octet serenades those who sit
through weddings and funerals
on the straight birch benches
of Lowville Mennonite Church,
just the way their parents
sang in the congregation
on Sunday mornings, their voices
sweep paint brushes

along the white washed walls
with more color than eyes
could ever see. And we should have known
that folks who once all wore
that same cut dress, the same plain coat
couldn't also sing in unison.
Somehow it had to be told that
we are not all made alike.

Pulling Taffy with Mom

We stretch out the pearly white
cord, forcing the candy taut
in both directions. Our hands meet
again in the middle. We tug. Its texture
thickens and tears. Mom tells me
how she used to do this
at Lewis County Mennonite youth parties,
a collection of shy girls in prayer coverings
and guys smelling of cows
they just milked, pulling until the taffy
is stiff and brittle. We cut. Small pieces

scatter on the kitchen counter.
Mom says that after she cut her hair,
turning the back of her cropped curls
on those bishops' teachings about length
and beauty, she could reach the high notes
of hymns better. As the sweets harden,

Mom recalls how she and her siblings
would meet in the haymow after a day
of cutting and driving tractors.
They'd build a labyrinth of bails
and travel this maze until the sun dropped
below the paneless windows,
until she crawled holes through
her thick wool stockings. We take a bite
and smile over a bowl full
of tastes, stony and sweet.

Picking Fruit

He trusts nature, like every blade
of grass, every flowering bush
is a member of the family. Like
his grandfather, who with a bag
of bread and cheese, walked him
along the Danube River
Saturday mornings to introduce him
to edible leaves and berries.
He'd return home late, full
of *kupine* and *shljive*. He can't find

those plants here. Like his language
and university degree, they're foreign
to this country. He makes friends
with other plants in the local park.
He gets close enough to the pines
for a kiss, smelling their needles
as if the odor spoke a language
only he understood. But on early summer
mornings when clouds calm
the sun's heat, those days when people
around here go strawberry picking,
he bakes dark bread that still
doesn't put an ounce around
his lean Balkan ribs.

Silent Territory

Tears for the men and women
who leave the places that know them.
—Naomi Shihab Nye

My grandfather wouldn't speak to his children
in German. His transition to English
was too full of misunderstandings and embarrassing
accents to turn back. Upon my request,
Mom dredges up the words for bread
and morning chores. Everything else is lost.

My husband abandoned his mother's Romanian
for the language he'd need in school. Now he clings
to every foreign phrase he learns
as if he'll find something
he misplaced between the new words.

With language absent, I have left
the town of my birth, the clothes
of my ancestors. The family farm
was sold to strangers years ago.
We don't plan for children,
having nothing left to bequeath them.

With Apologies to my Hometown

I have not forgotten the way home, north
through whiteout or moonless sky.
Nor is it deficient gratitude
that keeps me away. Love alone can't save
this relationship. It is fortitude I lack.

To settle there, you must swell
with hot springs and strut across winter
like a wild turkey. You must take
to murky skies with the free force
that compels snow off rooftops and rest
on the sleeping ground like a whisper.

You can never pull your roots
up above the frozen earth, not even
for one taste of the fresh air. Those roots
will instinctively reach for warmer ground
with a drive as powerful as lust.

Lewis County Chronicle 3

Marian didn't care if others
thought it improper.
She knew better than to let pass
the chance to sit in the front row
with the men, pretending
she had completed high school
and her education hadn't ended
at thirteen. She hid her hands, callused
from washing wool in the Indian River,
cutting meat from winter pigs,
and raking the corners of hay fields. She forgot
about the silent farmhands she cooked for
and the raw stench of horseshit
they tracked in, or the time she had to pay
a sitter for the lawyer's boys she nannied
to go to a wedding supper. She didn't even
begrudge her rare weekend off
when she could attend youth group hymn sings.
Instead, she thought of the days
she had played "teacher" with her sister,
the way the chalk tablet had rested
in her hands, and how happy she was
the times her father had allowed her
to write the names of newborns
in the family Bible, the extravagant
curve of letters. What if this
six-week Bible course was four years,
and she'd return home
with a gold-sealed degree

to hang on the wall of a schoolhouse
with an indoor restroom and furnace
rumbling in the basement,
instead of the hand-written certificate
and opportunity to teach Bible
to women or children on Sundays?

A Blasphemy

A girl attacked me once with a number 2 Eagle pencil
for a whiny lisping impression of a radio preacher
—Rodney Jones, "A Blasphemy"

Yes, I stabbed him. I don't deny that.
When he started imitating that voice
I've heard too often before.
That voice, like my father, my pastor,
that preacher on the radio. Like Paul
and Timothy telling me to be silent,
to submit. For that moment, I thought
I was in Europe, four hundred years ago,
tied to a burning stake for knowing something
about birth control. But *it was still*
Tuscaloosa, late summer. And however
different I had hoped he was,
he wasn't. He was no different from any
of the three billion men in *the world forever.*
I waited for him to holler or flinch,
any sense that I had gotten through. But that
would have been like an Orthodox priest
admitting women can step behind
the alter. Or an Amish bishop
sitting next to his wife, next to any woman
for that matter, during worship. In the end I did
what any self-respecting girl would do:
I washed his wound. I covered it
with white, clean gauze. And I let him go
back into the world—hoping the blood

would rise up, dotting through his bandage—
as I stayed behind in my bedroom
with my anger burning so hot
it peeled the paper off the walls.

Where We Start

There is a pet bird on my hand, one claw tucked, as well as
his beak. I sit like a Madam Tussaud wax statue. Soon my hand
will join him in sleep. What brings me to this kind of sacrifice?
Is this about scrubbing the bathroom sink before pink fuzz ap-
pears around the faucet, laundry day? Is it about my husband
setting the breadmaker on the edge of the counter, mouth open
for me to fill?

Eve searched days past the tree line where Adam stopped
clearing. She called *Lilith* until her throat was too raw to whis-
per. No answer. She returned to the house he covered with palm
leaves, sewed together skins and feathers. Her back slumped by
the weight of a growing child, she dug weeds along side Adam
near harvest time. She pushed silent cries through childbirth,
Adam pulling the baby from her insides. Still, she didn't stop
her search for Lilith. Eve knew too well the curse of God—this
desire she felt for her husband. Her only comfort was to admire
the clear eyes of a woman brave enough to leave the only man
on earth.

What is folklore but correcting history gone awry?

On this day in 1900, the International Ladies Garment
Workers Union was founded. In a few days, it will be the birth
of the Ellen Kuzwayo, South Africa, 1914, listed not in the his-
tory books but my activist calendar to be tossed out at the end
of the year. But is this about the fodder for fable?

Or is it about how I let my bird walk across my keyboard,
how I clean up the extra letters he leaves behind while I read
that in Cairo 1922, Huda Shaarawi removed her veil in public?

Keeping Warm

To hell with these up-state New York lakes
that freeze so hard every winter
you can drive a hockey puck
or car across them. Who says it's the kind
of place you never leave? But if you do
the cold clings to you
like icicles to a roof ledge—your nose
never warms. I took him there

to walk down the middle
of the road, no one driving through
the afternoon I pointed out my old window,
around the back of the gray
shingled house—the one
with the yellow cushioned window seat
over the garden and playhouse-on-stilts
that my mother painted with Bambi
and Donald Duck—next to the apple tree
and the two with poisonous berries
that fed the chickadees
through starved winters
but died themselves. His arm around me

at the convenience store where I worked
between semesters, I dug into three scoops
of Rocky Road while he warmed himself
with coffee in the booth next to the hotdogs
sweating out their last moments in their miniature
glass sauna. It didn't feel like summer

to him. He wants to move south
to Florida. What do I know

about that kind of constant heat? I know
lazy maple leaves that change
color in August, two months grown
and ready to quit. And rough-skinned apples
that fall to the ground so cold
you need gloves to pick them. Filthy hills
of snow sticking it out through April.
Not a damn thing about leaves
that hold to a branch year round

or an eternity of morning kisses.
I know about the way they stop, like leaves
falling so quietly you don't notice
until the tree is half bare.

II

Paradise
Revised

Ars Poetica

We're all here, knocking
together like unlucky
nightclub dancers, sweating
under our clothes for the sound
of words. We all crave
the way poetry teases us
from the page, our despondent hope
that its flirtation is sincere.
Our spouses may keep their vows
through the tough times, but poetry
lets us down. It betrays us
over and over again—slipping
into the writer's house down the street.
We fight. It leaves. We sit on the couch
with a tub of Death
by Chocolate, watch rented
romance movies, lament. But it returns
to beg. Like snared lovers, we open
the door, take it into our arms, remember
our many late nights, ask
for no explanation.

Funeral Address for an Ex-Boyfriend

The hospital window views a courtyard
and youthful grass cut by a lawnmower's
blade. The bed sits gray and tired
like an old man's face. I imagine
I wait for you there, the way my father waited
for my mother, thirty years
after their wedding. After three children,
the house they built with cathedral
ceilings, the Miata and hot tub.

But Mom lived. In this story, the doctor
shakes his head. And I mourn for you.
I accept flowers and sympathy cards. I write
thank you notes for half-eaten
meals. I pretend we have this kind
of relationship. Not how it ended
with me running like the Israelites
out of Egypt. Not how your pharaoh charm
brought me only plagues: addictions,
women, motorcycles. Not your mighty
squint of eyes smiling down on me
like a blasphemous cow and how still
I think you could have led me to Canaan.

But I am not without hope. I mourn now
because on the day you die I'll be shopping
for avocados or arranging
freshly cut tulips. The woman
who holds you in death, she is the one
who will cry over her wilderness
of lost years.

Not a Poem for my Uncle

There is no one in my family
who jumped off a bridge,
who turned on the gas and lay down.
Nor have I needed to be tranquilized
by *Miltown*, listening to the music
that swam about Anne Sexton's head.
There's only the haziest story

of a great uncle
committed by his siblings. I tried
to write about that once
but it was the men I loved
who formed my stanzas of angst.
Now with you, there are

no lines of self-pity, no flaunting
my martyrdom, no escapes
of biblical proportion. With you,
I wake in a bed full of window light.

Since you have all the other answers,
tell me—as you ogle CNN
while food molds on the heap
of dishes you claim you'll wash
before you pull out of the driveway
at daybreak—what am I to write?

Night Fright

On a whim, we took her
from the pet store, debating names
and wing clipping for the drive home.
He wants her to fly from one end
of the apartment to the other
in some kind of native freedom
that he's sure speaks to a bird's soul.
My childhood pet flew out the door
in winter and all of the evidence
supports clipping that I found researching the web
where I read of the disorienting fear
that wakes us at two in the morning to her
screeching, a baby's cry, as she flaps
against her cage bars, tossing blood
and feathers. I speak in my calm voice, open
the cage door for her to tumble out
on the floor. At a dinner party
the next evening, he will talk of how he
understands her, like when he
would wake in the dark under the guns
of the small Yugoslavian Navy boat
that guarded the Danube River. After he left
that boat, he left that country and then another
to end up here, where I don't want him
to ever leave. But now on the couch
in this lighted room, the three of us
breath alike—an uneven tempo—
as she picks the red from her feathers,
and I want to confess that I imagine
his death, and me curled up in some corner
of my loneliness, when he's late
driving home from work, all the details

down to the phone call I can't make
to his parents, only able to say
Zvonko nije ovde, that he is not
here, somehow needing
to mourn now as if mourning then
won't be enough. And so we argue
until we exhaust the matter of wings.

Lewis County Chronicle 4

Beef rice soup, potato salad
and white cake. The rush
of Niagara Falls and the quiet coffee
on her sister's porch, Allen and Marian
listened to brother-in-law Emanuel
tell stories unsuitable for bedtime
about World War I C.O. life
in Fort Leavenworth. How he ate
hard cornbread and preferred
locked cells. How he quoted
Romans 12:19, "Do not take revenge,
but leave room for God's wrath,"
to those who called him yellowback.
How a Hutterite boy, handcuffed to the bars
so his heals couldn't touch the floor, gave
a fresh apple from home to the sergeant.
How one Brethren was put in a pen
with a vicious dog who only licked
his hand, the way Daniel was saved
from the mouth of lions. How his mother's
prayers saved him from everything
but a cesspool dunking. How he still
got sick some nights.

A year later with the birth of their first son,
Marian had not heard the Jewish saying
that it is bad luck to name a child
after the living. But when she watched
this boy carry his two-year-old brother
down the aisle of a mourning church
eleven years later, when she saw him
negotiate milk prices, manage

hired hands, and fix broken beams
in the barn—swinging a hammer
just as his father once had—she grieved
the sacrifices of the few named Emanuel.

INS Interview

He's home with a cold,
unsettled in his chest like squirrels
in an attic, but it won't stop him
from bending the outcome
of the wars. It's reinventing
the enemy's language,
this eager choice at his age
to drop down to a part-time
job and a class schedule.
He's a vegetarian, unlike
his brother or father, unlike most men
of any time. It's a sporting life—
trying to capture scenic photos
instead of blood or meat.
His landscape is cluttered
with burning gallon drums, grain
bundles, bodies of secrets and vintage
stories of revenge. It's a constant search
for his name in print
in the phonebook, on an electric bill—
any witness to say he's still a part
of some society. *Look at the wild
blue sky,* he tells me. *Take time
to number the dandelions.*
They will replace
the album of memories
he carries. They will turn
this hiding place into ordinary time.

A Different Kind of War Story

A mile from Fort Drum on the way to church,
we drove past tanks or trucks covered
with camouflaged men and canvas
the color of ripened figs. We learned to sleep
through the clap of planes breaking
the sound barrier and packed the trunk
with jars on Saturday mornings to park
next to the rich pastures of old barn yards
now gouged into dust covered tank tracks
in search of wild berries, small and hard
like blue pellets, spread on both sides
of the barbed wire and restricted
bombing-area postings, growing
between vengeance and forgiveness.
As the fear of a Russian nuclear death
diffused, our high school basement
bomb shelter turned to dust, all canned foods
and toiletries emptied, just a lone mattress
where classmates snuck down to make out.
Once a year, we lined up in the gym
next to a table of empty ammo shells
under an instructional video about a boy
who finds a bomb in his back yard
and is smart enough to tell about it.
Uniformed men offered awkward mercy
as they drilled us on kinds of ammo
not to touch. Still, one time I ran my hand
along the edge of a bomb casing,
which left its blue ink still pressed
into the grooves of my fingertips.

Thoughts After Hearing a Lecture on Translation

How is it that he loves me
through all of these languages,
through the check points
and road blocks of Serbo-Croatian,
German, sometimes Romanian,
the dictionaries he strums through
while I'm fast asleep, while
the introduction to his language—
the book I bought
with good intentions—rests
beside me on my nightstand
and the gift from his brother
in Paris—40 lessons to speak
French—sits shelved? My three
months immersed in French
are ten years forgotten
except *Je ne comprend pas.*
My dreams are content
in one language
while his wide-eyed mind juggles
four tongues. And this is his gift to me—
how he can love someone
so lazy, so rested
in American English—this language
of our love, this language
so far from his fractured home.

What It Doesn't Say in the Brochure

There are no amusement parks
with over-heated employees
dressed as chocolate kisses
or quilt shops staffed by women
in black bonnets. You can't find
covered bridges or playhouses
boasting live animals. There is no good
reason to visit this place
unless you find enchantment
in everyday objects
and plain language, unless
you cry over pet hamsters
buried in Legg's eggs
between the leaning walls
of garages or like
your entire back yard tilled
into a garden. Otherwise,
cancel the plane ticket. Unpack
the car. There is nothing else
to show you in this town
where neighbors meet
for stroller walks and it's front page news
when the son of the football coach
vandalizes the grocery store's
soda machine—taking a hatchet to it
like he wanted to hit his father
those nights his mother had to
hide her eyes behind sunglasses.
I didn't say nothing happened—
just nothing unusual. Plant your own
hard-to-care-for roses
in smelling distance

of your neighbors.
Have a funeral for the goldfish.
Carve your tree stump
into a giant squirrel or beer bottle.
Make a vacation of your own town.

To my Yugoslavian In-Laws

If we could speak,
I would tell you that we have
trees here too, and rivers.
I know how to hammer
a nail. Transatlantic phone calls
are expensive, even for us
with our two cars, dishwasher
and American salaries. That he
will not get lazy or forget
about the ways he needed to make money
during the war, the merchandise
exchanged in dark corners of Turkey.
He is still thankful for good health.
He passes on every kiss
you tell him to give me.
I would admit that he misses
the stone beaches of the Adriatic,
he accepts the Atlantic's murky water
as part of the compromise. He thinks
Lancaster's streets are too vacant
at night and there is no place
to ride a bike. Also, that I wouldn't take
your name and will never
believe the wine in the cup
turns to blood. That he and I can't
agree on a slipcover for the couch.
That there is no perfect place
for anyone.

Still-life with Office Worker

This room has no windows.
It is where invention begins
with its office painting:
a blend of blues, pinks, yellows,
and greens—almost the water lilies
of Monet, almost his cluttered garden
and landscape of lovers. My husband

wants me to replace it
with something modern—rigid lines
and static circles. But my daily life
is this impression
of an impression, a plastic
flower arrangement, or the faux

brick face of a building. I want
the painting in the hallway
with the seagulls and blowing
sand dunes to drown out the rattle
of the copier machine. My frantic work

is not dedication but the search
for the balance of a butterfly
landing on a maple leaf, the temperature
of the water off the Gulf coast
of Florida, or the wry belief
that the sun still survives outside
these walls, painted
the color of skinned bone.

Postulates

If I lived near the ocean, owned a swimsuit for every day of the week, like underwear to remember it was Sunday or Monday...learned to dig clams with my toes...walked the sand with a metal detector, ignoring the peering vacationers; then I'd have more use for limbs other than my hands.

If I were a super model, 5'11" and none-of-your-business weight...drank malt chocolate shakes to throw up in the restaurant bathroom, no matter who sold the story to a gossip magazine...sued them or interviewed with *People* about how I beat the habit, quit drugs, learned to love my inner-child and posed for the cover; then I'd have other ways to lie.

If I still lived in Philadelphia, New York, managed the local convenient store...openly admitted I watched Days of Our Lives, As the World Turns, Guiding Light in succession on my days off in a prefab house...two kids, a divorce and never missed a high school basketball game; then I'd have no use for pretension.

If I won night club contests, wet t-shirt or twisting, big enough to award a medium-size trophy and certificate...favorite drink known by the people who hung out there and cared where I got my hair cut, what perfume I wore...my own bar stool world view; I might imagine my name on places other than a page.

Instead, alone on Friday nights...my fingers scarred from catching fire...I need to pour out language burning in my throat.

The Art of Taking

I write that this rough Balkan boy,
scarred from a street fight, is scared
of heights and won't ride
roller-coasters. He cried during
the phone call to his mother
on our wedding day and messes-up
the order of English swear words.
I admit he watches

live cop shows. And when I tire
of his secrets, I write about my modest
regard for the unsmiling photos
of his church bishops, who vow
to never give in to the taste of steak
nor whisper to a lover after release.
Though this didn't save his friend
from dying in a monastery
of a disease no one would name
aloud. I retell the stories his friends

exchange over fruit pies
at dinner parties: the casual stroll
to the theatre as if the shells popping
along Sarajevo's streets
were merely firecrackers,
the trip into Austria
hidden under train seats,
and the self-imposed wound

to avoid the front lines. I hardly trouble
to seek forgiveness for what
I expose, claiming his whole country

as my writing field and supposing I can add
more truth than the stains
the bullets have left. These are not
mere plums of information,
tasty juice splashed onto a page.

On Writing a Truthful Poem

Speak the truth, but leave immediately after.
—Slovenian Proverb

This room is full of your parents, siblings, aunts, and dead grandmothers. It is filled with the minister who baptized you, your mother's second cousin once removed, the guy who butchered your grandfather's beef. They've decided on the truth. It is oyster stew for Christmas dinner, Johnny Cake every breakfast. It is the farm in West Martinsburg and how early spring in the sugar bush taught the value of hard work. It is communion and foot-washing every four months. It is games of Dutch Blitz and Rook, swimming among the leaches in Beaver Lake. It is learning how to lay topsoil so that rain doesn't wash it away to reveal the dirt. It is hiding your sins deep in your pockets. It is not for you to challenge or interpret. It is why your family could stop loving you with the flip of a page, the reading of one word, the switching of one fact. It is why they might get questioned by the grocery store clerk (who went to church camp with your cousin) or why the milk truck driver might start looking at them funny. This room is full. No one waits for you outside.

Lewis County Chronicle 5

Returning home, Marian sewed
curtains from fabric
used as tablecloths for the wedding.
Allen shoveled manure at his father's
farm on the Number Three Road.
Those were the fall months—the plowing
and seeding complete, the silos full,
the months when dinner did not have
to wait, only feeding and milking to do
before the days when the blowing
snow would make it treacherous
just to cross the street to the barn.
Those were the carefree months,
when it was still possible to drive
the roads to church, Allen holding
Marian's hand even when he needed to shift.

Marian sat on one side of the aisle,
Allen on the other like any given
Sunday. But that day, six Bibles lined
the front table, and one hid the paper
quoting Proverbs 16:33, "The lot is cast
into the lap, but its every decision
is from the Lord," meant to miraculously
turn a mere man into a minister. Of the six men
called forward, Allen looked
into the drained eyes and deep lines
on the forehead of his father,
now a bishop, and chose that Bible,
cold to his touch, to become
the ordained, and with his wife
stepped into the first chill of winter.

Fat Tuesday

Dough and lard fry
to bring on the season
of sacrifice. Our friend jokes
that she'll give up celibacy
as we eat *fasnachts* to fill
our stomachs with what Lent
will not allow. I am tempted
by a need to prepare
for anything. To fortify my life
like Noah readying for the flood.
Because the truth is

famine does not only appear
when the church requires it.
Other Fat Tuesdays are hard
to admit—our legs intertwined
during sleep, shared morning coffee.
They masquerade as signs
of Spring, not of the emptiness
that could follow, lasting much longer
than merciful Lent.

Paradise Revised

Marriage wasn't born
when they saw each other
nakedly perfect and said
This is good. When all they had
to do was name things
and choose between
Winesap or McIntosh. That love
was a drug straight to the heart
and they got lazy,
turning on each other with just
a couple of whispered, serpentine
agitations. Then came her pain

and his bossiness. Beating
the earth to feed the kids.
Sewing circles around breasts
and bellybuttons. When they could

no longer blame the snake
or God, when all they had
to look forward to was feeding
their bodies back to the dust, marriage
was born, as scorched by flaming
swords, they passed through
to another kind of paradise,
clinging.

Two Mothers and a Baby

I listen to his sleep talk
in a language I say I'll learn
someday, about Albanians chasing him
through his elementary school
and, as dreams go, the devil
in an army uniform. It is years since
he walked the uneven streets
of Belgrade, one shoulder balancing
Serbia, Bosnia dragged by his right leg.
Solomon's counsel would have
cut his body in two, half flung over
the border, while I watched
starved men stare through barbed wire
into my TV and wondered
on which side the ones like him
ended up, the ones with blood
of enemies mixed together
in the cavities of their hearts. At least
he ended up on the right side
of my bed. And I, raised in a town
where all that threatened us
were flies in old cow feed, wake him
from his night thrashings and wonder if,
even as I say it, I understand.

My Husband Becoming a Naturalized Citizen

He raises his hand, as if to say stop
to a man facing him with a gun.
And really, it is a shotgun wedding.
He's committing *I do* to this country
that can never be his true love.
He will always remember the country
that first rocked him in her bosom,
who in the end, turned her whole body away
with such violence that the force flew him
across an ocean. He's had a common reaction,
declaring his hatred for her, that he'd never
go back, even if she begged him.
But she is still the location
of his dreams in the candor of night.

Some party invitations are better left refused.
No one wants to witness the uncomfortable steps
of a newlywed who would rather be dancing
with someone else. Sooner or later he'll squirm
within her touch like a man
in a poorly fitted suit. Still, his legs
slowly sway to the music's rhythm.
He tries out a dip and flirtatious turn.
His nimble body settles into the moves
that will accompany the years ahead.

III
LOSING
GROUND

Lewis County Chronicle 6

God is my retreat and strength,
and is always with me.
Though the load of the farm is like a full silo on my back
    and the ministry's a job for a smarter man,
        I will not begrudge the command of scripture
        that I serve just one master.
Though I must rise by 2:00 for morning devotions
    and wake my son at 5:00
        to disrupt the cows from their slumber.
        A boy, who at age eight, burned out
        the engine in the truck, driving it
        through uncleared pasture and prairie dog holes.
Though the hay in the field rots like a fresh carcass
    while the churches fight as trapped foxes,
        and baby John's hungry cries are yet
        to wake Marian from her convalescing,
I will not be tired.
I will let a smaller farm
    and sermons titled "The Battle of Life"
        pierce a beat back into this heart.
And pray another hour of sleep
    will raise me from this mortal bed.

The Cost of a Garden Plot at City Park

Forty grandchildren raised
on sun-dried apples, ham
in the smokehouse and five colors
of roses, and none of us could prevent
the shrinking creek and milk prices,
the farm handed over
to a family from Pennsylvania
who climbed the silo to repaint
Zehrdale to Herrdale, tore off
the stucco wallpaper,
and ripped out the wall between
the kitchen and grandpa's study
as if the stained-glass windows
in the sun room, the blueberry patch
and toboggan hill always existed
just for them, as if they planned to stay.

But now, again the barn is vacant.
This new family, like others along
Lowville's gravel roads, packs boxes
fat with dreams of a shorter winter,
a growing season long enough
for three cuttings, and a quick drive
to a shopping mall. They advertise
in Lancaster County papers,
"Upstate New York farmland.
Get away from the congestion."

Now it's only Amish
who pay drivers to move
their households north—their horses
pulled in trailers behind them. Only Amish

who want these summers too short
for a tourist season and the land
rocky enough to teach
virtues of work and hope.
One farm after the next has cut
the electric wiring to the house
while its occupants write letters
in candlelight to relatives still living
the comfortable yet crowded life
in states farther south.

We drive past and I point out
the tree we used to climb,
the part of the creek that was once
deep enough to swim in,
and the tractor we climbed off
still sitting empty in the fields,
while a man in black suspenders
passes it with his team of large-hoofed
horses reviving the forsaken soil.

Migraines and Other Mennonite Pains

Forgive your parents for marrying cousins whose parents married cousins. Don't run track or vote or swear oaths or take jury duty (if you can help it). Don't act proud or pretty. Memorize every tortured drawing in the *Martyrs' Mirror*. Put on hand-sewn trousers or cape dresses. Don't marry a Catholic. Pray to Jesus like he is your best friend. Know what it means to be a disciple. Dirk Willems knew (burned to death after saving his captor). Love your enemies. Convert disciples (but not those with new ideas). Keep your hands in fruitful soil, and wake by dawn for milking. Don't step beyond the invisible line drawn in the bishop's dirt. Sit through long sermons on wooden benches. Lijsken Dircks endured more than that (drowned the day after birthing a son). Pick up your cross and shoulder it. Get tied to the stake, dumped head first into cesspools, laughed at for wearing a dress with sneakers. Read the Bible in English and some kind of German. Know what it says and follow every letter. The pain is nothing you can't stand.

A foolish fox is caught by one leg,
but a wise one by all four.
—Serbian Proverb

In her dreams
her cats speak English.
She calls their front legs
arms. Paws, hands.
They're named for Pedro
and Elena, two kids she used to see
at the corner Laundromat—probably
college age now. She doesn't care
what people say,
that no man wants a woman
with more than one cat.
She has stopped her search
for the lost coin, missing sheep,
the rib she pulled from her side
at his request—her attempt to make
him whole again. He has become
an archetype—the one you always believe
when he swears off booze
or one night stands. The type
who pushes back the wedding date,
cleans out the bank account and slips down
a road with no name on a holiday weekend
or slips into a woman
whose name you know too well.
She finds no shame
in the nights she spends with cat
in lap or mending the wound

in her side like darning
a wool sock. She believes
what the Slovenians say,
"Only lend to a friend
what you cannot afford to lose."

After the Divorce
for Curt

Normandy is beautiful this time
of year but that didn't stop
the Allied planes from bombing Caen
for its liberation. On the university square
is a carved phoenix, like the city,
rising from the flames. That must be
how you feel some days—walking
through ravaged streets, wiping
the ashes from your feet.

But think of your soul
as William's Cathedral;
having already stood a thousand years,
it will survive this rubble falling
around it. And you will return
to that majestic beauty
like the Conqueror himself
from the hill of Hastings,
to kiss its stone floor
before joining the others dancing
atop his chateau walls.

Losing Ground

We returned from Ocean City in March
with photos of snow sifting through sand.
In the end, the long winter tested
the resolve of us all. After the first few storms,
the beaches gave in, allowing the wind
and snow to pull the sand with them
into the ocean's depth. No numbers
of jetties or sand dunes could stop
the wearing away, leaving
a sudden decline to the shore.

He says I should be happy because
my sorrow only brings him grief.

Now June, I slide into Rehoboth's surf
that still bites from the winter's chill.
My heart has always beat with the rhythm
of this place—its quiet side streets,
relaxed boardwalk, and porch-front
restaurants. And now, I share its sense
of disappearance. Sure, there are times
of joy, times when I can kiss him
without feeling the sting of what
commitment takes. But it is not long
before the end of this day and the drive home
through Route 1's heavy traffic, salt
thinning the skin that swathes my bones.

Note in a Bottle

I can no longer remember the name
of the café in Black Mountain,
North Carolina where I passed time
one summer. The coffee drinkers
around me swapped hitch-hiking stories
and how many times they'd been arrested
for marijuana, but I just stared
at the fresh faces of the Seven Sisters
Mountain Range. It is no wonder
people with something to hide go there.
A mountain is not interested
in intimacy. To get close, you must
overcome abrupt climbs and jagged
boundaries, only to meet an icy tip.
In the end, I looked to a far-too-young man
for friendship. A month later, the boy
admitted he always wanted an Italian-looking
lover. The sandy color of my hair
was more of a compromise
than he could make. Still, we crossed
the border into Tennessee one night so he
could say he'd been there. I should have
driven alone in the other direction
toward the shore instead. It is the ocean
that knows how to receive a person
with yielding sand and waves
that come up to greet you, softened
by the years of water embracing stone.

Lewis County Chronicle 7

There was no farewell, no last
words. Only a silent man still
in bed after morning chores
should have been completed.
Only mourners with casseroles,
quoting to Marian the words of a song
Allen had requested at church
the day before, "Ask the Savior
to help you, comfort, strengthen,
and keep you." Only hired help
to assist with the farm for a fee
and two rooms upstairs. Only
a rotting barn the condoling inspector
condemned once the chicken house
was built. Only years of chicken stench,
picking out the eggs with blood clots
for her morning breakfast. Passing
his devotional books onto his sons
and grandsons as they turned the age
of his picture on her bed stand. Only
bus trips with sister Esther to Nova Scotia
and Michigan, hours of knitting
until her glaucoma set in, then the radio
on whose waves her evening praise songs
would ride into the advancing night.

Kitchen on Antwerp Street

The room is long and thin
like a diner car, though
the food isn't as greasy
or good. Appliances
line up against the wall.
An alcove holds a table
with orange vinyl benches
where a girl sits,
after the others have finished.
She is staring at the nine peas
still occupying her plate,
the total of her age, a pea added
after each birthday.
The dog walks past
his food bowl to stare
at the cookie jar. Kids outside
play Kick the Can. There is a door
to escape to the back porch.
The garden is beyond
where the same girl torched
a stuffed clown who kept
tempting her to suck her thumb,
like an Anabaptist martyred
for someone else's sins.

How to Show Decay Without Filming a Rotting Carcass

There are so many options: a pale horse
meandering through abandoned streets,
a lone seagull picking at empty sand.

Or how about a prime minister shot
in a country whose sewers ooze
with brutality's waste? Tribute flowers
set in place for the funeral march
catch fire from the mourning candles
held up by sand heaped along the sidewalks.
Wax seeps into the street, crowded with armored
men. Bystanders cover their ears
from the cruelty of the gun salute.

Or just notice the crumbling brick of a city
once cradled by a wide-eyed nation
and the soda bottles replacing fish
in the Conestoga River. With no sense
of decorum, their scaly remains flop
upon my doorstep. My neighbors and I
have learned to ignore the stench—sealing
our windows shut, pulling the blinds,
and switching the TV channel
to a reality show with bikini clad women
eating the eyeballs of lambs.

Rush Hour

I feel that I should write
about farming while cows graze
near trees they're cutting down
along our end of route 30.
Orange cones like homeless men
line up with *The world is going to end*
warning signs of single lane
congestion and prediction
of a better future. These days
with my body hollowed into the gray
vinyl seat of my Toyota coupe,
I've learned the harmonies to every
Indigo Girls' tune. Not bad
in itself but my hands lie dormant
too long for the daughter
of farmers. Only one generation away,
I'm close enough to listen
patiently through NPR newscasts
of farmers dumping milk.
But I've only experienced
that tourist kind of farming—Sundays
in my grandmother's raspberry patch,
a mouth stained with sweetness.
I think about farming
the way I dream of Alaska,
fancying self-sufficient mountains
where I'd need only a satellite dish
and cell phone. Meanwhile, my brother
and father disagree on the intelligence
of cows. I tend to side with my dad.
Wandering the same fields,
eating the same food, letting anyone

pull at their teats. All lined up straight
for milking like the desks of a typing pool.
Cattle shoots. That's why I feel
like writing a farming poem
about a single tractor and the man
driving it through open acres
past every packed highway of America.

Video from Bosnia

There is a body bound
in white cloth on an outdoor cot
amid crying women
wearing *dimije* and scarves.
Even during communist times,
it was the same. My husband answers
my questions about the lack of casket
and the demure women—his mother,
the only Serbian Orthodox there,
stands out in pants with head uncovered.
But he prefers to point out
where a house once stood, the walk
to the stream for water, how gray
his father's hair has become, and that even
the imam smokes (he having given up
the habit years ago). He translates pieces
of the elegy on sorrow, going
to paradise, and thinking about life—
the same speech in any religion—
until the men proceed down the hill,
trading the weight of the body
every few steps, and my husband's father
lowers himself down the hole
to lay his friend into the earth
after a life of war and heavy drinking.
Then the video switches to weeks before
and the man alive sitting in the dirt yard
where he will later lie, surrounded
by family, shade trees, and plum brandy.
He laughs, his face red with high
blood pressure. My husband says,
Isn't the landscape beautiful?

The Library in Philadelphia, New York

Its size has not changed
since my childhood with books yellowing
the eight-foot walls of the first floor
of a corner house. The second floor is filled
with filmy pictures of the old bakery and ribbons
worn in the bicentennial parade.
It isn't a big place, like Sarajevo University
where after the whistle and shell explosion,
its library took a night and day
to burn. It's not like Mrs. Pennhollow's
down the street where for dolls, she reserved
one room alone. When I delivered
surplus beans from our garden, I'd unzip
the stuffed dog that sat on the chair
in the corner and free the stuffed puppies
crowded inside like a bomb shelter.
Locking dolls in glass cabinets
doesn't fill the hours in a day.
There is still time for risking a walk
across the railroad bridge or falling in love
with the wrong man. If Mrs. P. had filled
that room with books because she liked
the sound of the author's name, the cover
design or the smell of the pages,
what might have I pulled
from her shelves? Perhaps a fairytale
with the original tragic ending. Perhaps
that would have prepared me
for how this town, like Sarajevo,
has burned to the ground—the Eagle Hotel,
the post office where I used to wait
for the bus before their historic loss

was chronicled on local primetime news.
Perhaps it would have taught me
what its like to build a bunker
out of library shelves
for protection from sniper fire,
and for the lack of water, to watch
those floors of books turn to ash.

All Saints Day, Serbian Orthodox Church

I wonder about the weight
of those candles my husband places
in the sand near the church's floor
to pray for the dead. When I ask him
who he prays for, he says, "all of them,"
but I imagine that the flame burns
specifically for the classmate
he tried to talk out of going to the war,
his grandfather who told him stories
of a forest queen, or the monk
who died of AIDS—his loyalty
to them as certain
as when they were living.
Instead of admitting I have not yet learned
how to mourn, I stand softly
on the belief that there is nothing
anyone can do for the dead. Let them

bury themselves, Jesus said, but he still
pulled Lazarus from the grave, unable
to take his own advice when it came
to a friend. Maybe Jesus said it
to comfort those of us
who haven't yet needed to embrace
the dead with the living—no graves to visit,
no fires burning, still
untried and unproven.

Gap

At the Rockvale Outlets next to a patchwork quilt of color-co-ordinated socks, you cut me off in line to request directions to a restaurant where you might find some Amish or at least Mennonites. You—hoisted up by shopping bags from Mikasa, Hugo Boss, and Donna Karin—ask the cashier what it's like to live among them. Do the buggies get in the way? You're in my way of picking up a quick pair of cheap Gap jeans before I drive home in my husband's bull of a car. Me, a cheerleader in a short pleated skirt, voted most energetic of my senior class, who has never buried my blond, sometimes dyed copper, hair under a prayer covering. I watch *Star Trek*, own two cell phones, you ig-norant urban schmuck. I drank Chianti and danced to *Blue Moon* as a tattoo of a dove peaked out the shoulder of my sleeve-less wedding dress. And this is how some Mennonites cut our bangs short, sassy from an issue of *Celebrities Hairstyle*. I want to offer you a Pennsylvania Dutch obscenity or something else of the Mennonite experience you're not looking for—a conver-sation about the Reformation, how Jacob Ammon led a schism over shunning or the impact of reading *Martyrs' Mirror* on a child. But the Amish Farm Museum across the street only of-fers carriage rides through the covered bridge until five and the cashier just finished writing directions to the Good & Plenty Restaurant. Tonight you'll feast on creamed corn and Shoofly pie while I microwave my TV dinner into rubbery, stir-fried oblivion.

Long Distance

Here, I tell you, it rained
that determined kind of rain.
Each drop was a lover
of some morsel of earth, chasing
after it like the other night
when half way home from a friend's,
we ducked into the doorway
of Williams' Apothecary. When the rain,
like English soldiers,
marched across the street, we gave into it
and, filling our shoes, hopscotched
the puddles in the park. You tell me

you're nightmaring my face
and your ex-girlfriend's into one. The two
of us are braided together and swallowed
by a train heading far
from you. I ask if you've forgotten
that this suitcase I carry
is borrowed and drenched, that I brought
only two pairs of shoes? Like a bird,
always returning each season,
I travel light. I know the grace
of a well-made nest like a photo I saw

in the newspaper showing a male crane
landing on the back of his partner
somewhere on Spanish cliffs. He knew
that her long, thin legs would not buckle
from the force of his heavy perch. Cranes choose
a mate for life, clinging through winter
and summer migrations. I'm convinced

it's not all about propagating the species,
the necessity that one find food
while the other sits on the eggs. It comes down
to knowing, no matter who says it,
we will carry each other's weight.

Publication Acknowledgements

"Angel in the Blue Room" appeared in *DreamSeeker Magazine*.

"A Different Kind of War Story," "Lewis County Chronicle 1," "Rush Hour," and "With Apologies to my Hometown" appeared in *Mochila Review*.

"Diversity" appeared in *The Mennonite*.

"Fairytale" appeared in *Whiskey Island Magazine*.

"A foolish fox is caught by one leg, but a wise one by all four" appeared in *The Circle Magazine*.

"Gap" appeared in *MARGIE: The American Journal of Poetry*.

"How to Show Decay without Showing a Rotting Carcass" and "Losing Ground" appeared in *Avatar Review*.

"Keeping Warm" and "The Library in Philadelphia, New York" appeared in *Blueline*.

"Newspaper Headline Reads: Sacrificial Sheep Shoves Man to his Death" appeared in *Red River Review*.

"Night Fright" and "Silent Territory" appeared in *Ellipsis Magazine*.

"Video from Bosnia" appeared in *The Fourth River*.

The Author

Debra Gingerich was raised in a small town in upstate New York, near the Lewis County Mennonite community of her birth. She has since lived in Lancaster, Pennsylvania, and Philadelphia, Pennsylvania, before moving to Sarasota, Florida, where she currently works in communications and public relations.

Gingerich completed her undergraduate studies at Eastern Mennonite University and received an M.F.A. in Writing from Vermont College. Her poems and essays have appeared in *The Mochila Review, MARGIE: The American Journal of Poetry, Whiskey Island Magazine, The Writer's Chronicle,* and elsewhere.

Printed in the United States
74267LV00002B/22-54

9 781931 038393